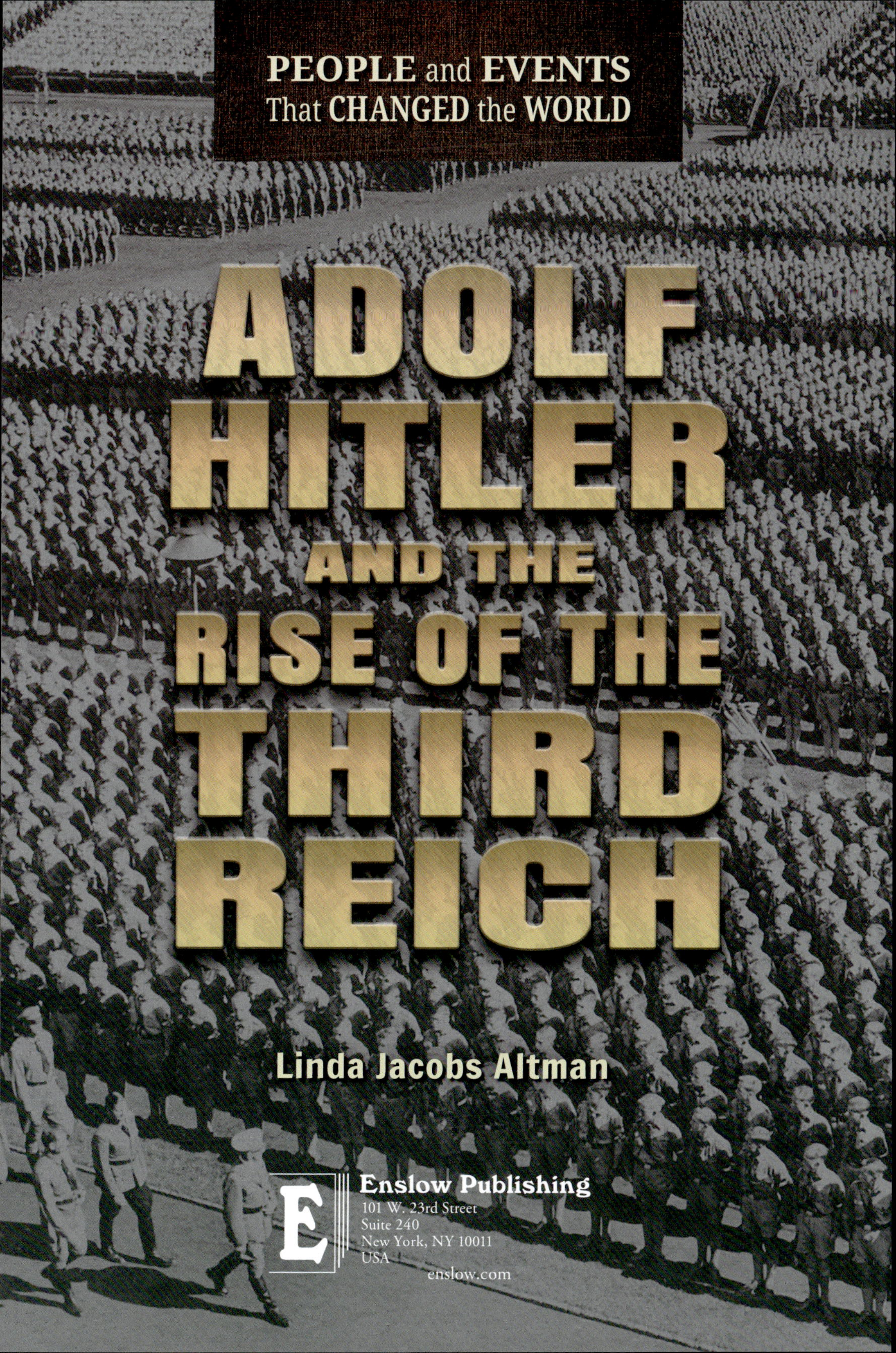

PEOPLE and EVENTS That CHANGED the WORLD

ADOLF HITLER AND THE RISE OF THE THIRD REICH

Linda Jacobs Altman

Enslow Publishing
101 W. 23rd Street
Suite 240
New York, NY 10011
USA
enslow.com

Published in 2016 by Enslow Publishing, LLC
101 W. 23rd Street, Suite 240, New York, NY 10011

Library of Congress Cataloging-in-Publication Data
Altman, Linda Jacobs, 1943- author.
Adolf Hitler and the rise of the Third Reich / Linda Jacobs Altman.
pages cm. — (People and events that changed the world)
Includes bibliographical references and index.
Summary: "Describes the geopolitical circumstances that led to the rise of Adolf Hitler and his Third Reich"— Provided by publisher.
ISBN 978-0-7660-7175-9
1. Hitler, Adolf, 1889-1945—Juvenile literature. 2. Heads of state—Germany—Biography—Juvenile literature. 3. National socialism—Juvenile literature. 4. Germany—History—1933-1945—Juvenile literature. 5. Holocaust, Jewish (1939-1945)—Juvenile literature. I. Title.
DD247.H5A8122 2016
943.086092—dc23
2015025535

Printed in the United States of America

To Our Readers: We have done our best to make sure all website addresses in this book were active and appropriate when we went to press. However, the author and the publisher have no control over and assume no liability for the material available on those websites or on any websites they may link to. Any comments or suggestions can be sent by e-mail to customerservice@enslow.com.

Portions of this book originally appeared in the book *Hitler's Rise to Power and the Holocaust.*

Photo Credits: Cover, pp. 3, 6, 26, 28, 49, 51, 65, 68, 71, 74, 87 ullstien bild/Getty Images; EdwardSV/Shutterstock.com (series logo background and headers throughout book), docent/Shutterstock.com (German flag on spine); pp. 9, 77 UniversalImagesGroup/Universal Images Group/Getty Images; p. 10 National Archives/Hulton Archive/Getty Images; p. 14 © Keystone Pictures USA/Alamy; pp. 19 Photo 12/Universal Images Group/Getty Images; p. 20 Hugo Jaeger/Timepix/The LIFE Picture Collection/Getty Images; p. 24 Universal History Archive/Universal Images Group/Getty Images; p. 31 Roger Viollet/Getty Images; pp. 36, 58 Keystone-France/Gamma-Keystone via Getty Images; pp. 38, 89 Keystone/Hulton Archive/Getty Images; p. 40 LAPI/Roger Viollet/Getty Images; p. 44, 62 Underwood Archives/Archive Photos/Getty Images; p. 46 Three Lions/Hulton Archive/Getty Images; p. 54 Imagno/Hulton Archive/Getty Images; p. 79 FPG/Archice Photos/Getty Images; p. 81 FPG/Hulton Archive/Archive Photos/Getty Images; p. 84 PhotoQuest/Archive Photos/Getty Images; p. 92 Central Press/Hulton Archive/Getty Images; p. 96 Thomas Trutschel/Photothek/Getty Images.

CONTENTS

Adolf Hitler leads a meeting of the Reichstag in 1939.

Introduction

In the 1930s, Adolf Hitler and his National Socialist German Workers' (Nazi) Party took power in Germany. As *Führer*, or leader, Hitler turned Germany into a police state. He then proceeded to violate treaties, break promises, and take territories that belonged to other countries.

The nations of Europe did everything they could to avoid war. Then Hitler went too far. On September 1, 1939, German troops invaded Poland. Two days later, Britain and France declared war on Germany. World War II had begun.

Hitler vowed to destroy his enemies and build a German *Reich*, or empire, that would last for a thousand years. This new, Nazi world would be populated by a "master race" of Northern Europeans, or Aryans, as he called them. He considered non-Aryans, such as Jews, Gypsies, Poles, Russians, and people of color, to be inferior. They would be given no rights in his Reich. Some would be exterminated, or killed. Others would be kept alive only so long as they served their Aryan masters. It was a dark and terrible vision that cost millions of lives.

In the early days of the war, Germany seemed unbeatable. One nation after another fell to the German *blitzkrieg*, or "lightning war." The Nazis conquered Poland in just twenty-six days. Denmark, Norway, Belgium, the Netherlands, and France fell in the spring of 1940. By the end of the year, the Germans had occupied most of Western Europe and made alliances with Italy and Japan. The Axis, as this alliance was called, soon conquered parts of Asia, Eastern Europe, and North Africa.

In 1941 the picture changed. In June, Germany invaded the Soviet Union, now called Russia. America entered the war on December 7, when Japan attacked the United States naval base in Pearl Harbor, Hawaii. The Germans soon found themselves fighting the British and the Americans in the West, and the Soviets in the East. They were also devoting men and resources to exterminating Jews and other people the Nazis saw as inferior.

Even when the war turned against Germany, this slaughter did not stop. Trains that could have carried troops and supplies to the fighting fronts were used instead to transport victims to death camps. The killing continued until the last possible moment.

After Germany surrendered on May 7, 1945, survivors began telling what they had suffered. Pictures of starving prisoners, mass graves, and gas chambers disguised as showers appeared in newspapers and movie newsreels. People all over the world were horrified.

As survivors told their stories, the horror grew. New words came into the language. Old words took on new meanings. *Holocaust* came to represent mass murder on a scale that had never been seen before. *Genocide* described the systematic killing of specific racial or ethnic groups.

Families, primarily mothers and children, arrive at Auschwitz concentration camp in 1942. Over a million people were killed at the camp, most of them in gas chambers.

Prisoners from a concentration camp in 1945. Not until the war ended that year did the world discover the true extent of the Holocaust and all of its horrors.

Introduction

These words are reminders of a grim truth—human beings can do terrible things to one another. This is why knowing about the Holocaust is so important. Knowledge is the best defense against the hatred that produced the Nazi racial state and caused the death of innocent millions.

CHAPTER 1

Germany and the First War

The end of World War I changed Germany forever. It had lost a bitter war and stood at the mercy of its enemies—the Allied nations, led by England, France, and the United States. Under the terms of surrender, the *kaiser*, or German emperor, gave up his throne. A new, democratic government known as the Weimar Republic took power, and promptly signed the armistice that stopped the fighting.

The German people were stunned. The military had been telling them that victory was close at hand. No enemy troops had invaded German soil or attacked German cities. To have lost was unthinkable. Many people called it a stab in the back. They believed that the new government had betrayed the nation.

A Harsh Treaty

In January 1919, Allied leaders gathered at Versailles, France. Their job was to create a permanent peace treaty. After a long and bloody war, many of these people wanted

World leaders gather at the Paris Peace Conference of 1919, which led to the Treaty of Versailles. From left to right: British Prime Minister David Lloyd George, Italian Premier Vittorio Orlando, French Premier Georges Clemenceau, and US President Woodrow Wilson.

to punish the Germans. The treaty they signed on June 28, 1919, was called the Treaty of Versailles.

This treaty stripped Germany of some of its territory and cut the size of its army. It made the German government pay over thirty billion dollars in damages to the Allies and accept all responsibility for starting the war.

Public reaction in Germany was swift. On the day the treaty was signed, it made the front page of *Deutsche Zeitung*, a popular newspaper: "Vengenace! German nation! Today . . . this disgraceful treaty is being signed. Do not forget it! . . . The German people will with unceasing labor, press forward to reconquer the place among nations to which it is entitled. Then will come vengeance for the shame of 1919."[1]

German democracy could not have begun under worse circumstances. Germans were used to an authoritarian government run by emperors and aristocrats. Many Germans feared democracy. But they also feared the Communism of the newly formed government in Russia. This government had grown out of the Russian Revolution of 1917 and eventually became the Union of Soviet Socialist Republics (USSR), or Soviet Union.

Under Communism in the Soviet Union, everything would belong to "the people" and be controlled by the government. Communism abolished private property and private enterprise.

To spread their form of government, the Communists called for worldwide revolution. In postwar Germany, many people were willing to listen. There was unrest in the nation, especially among war veterans. Not only had they been defeated in battle, many of them were out of work. They made a good audience for Communist ideas.

The Stab in the Back

After World War I, ultranationalists refused to accept that Germany was defeated on the battlefield. That did not fit with their belief that Germany was "invincible" and somehow more important than any other nation in Europe. Instead, they blamed the leaders of the new Weimar Republic for Germany's defeat. It was these leaders who had signed the treaty that stripped Germany of territory, limited the size of its military, and accepted full responsibility for starting the war. They had also agreed to pay billions of dollars in reparations for the damages the war had caused.

Field Marshall Paul von Hindenburg was the first to call this "betrayal" a stab in the back. He had picked up the term from a mistranslation of a book by British general Frederick Maurice.

It was only a matter of time before Adolf Hitler turned that term into a rallying cry for his struggle against the Weimar Republic and the treaty its leaders had signed.

Knowing this, the German army formed a special unit to investigate groups and people suspected of Communist beliefs. One of the men chosen for that unit was Adolf Hitler.

Hitler's Early Life

The man who would one day rule Germany was Austrian by birth. He was born on April 20, 1889, to Alois Hitler and his third wife, Klara. Adolf was the fourth of six children, but all of his older siblings died in infancy.

Adolf's father was born to an unmarried maid named Maria Schicklgruber. The identity of Alois's father is uncertain. But most likely it was Johann Heidler, the man Maria married when her son was five years old. When Alois became an adult, he took his father's name. However, he changed the spelling from "Heidler" to "Hitler."

If Alois Hitler had not changed his name, his son would have become "Adolf Schicklgruber." Hitler's enemies often made fun of this possibility. It was hard to imagine millions of people thrusting their right arms into the air and shouting, "Heil Schicklgruber."

Adolf Hitler had a difficult childhood. His father was demanding and critical. He expected his son to follow in his footsteps and work for the Austrian government. But young Hitler had bigger things in mind. First he wanted to be an artist. Then he wanted to be an architect. He failed at both.

After completing school Hitler moved to Vienna. There, he found himself drifting and alone. Rather than take a regular job, he lived from hand to mouth. He sometimes stayed in what would be called a homeless shelter today. To make money, he drew picture postcards and sold them on the streets.

Primary Source—Hitler's Failure as an Artist

Adolf Hitler liked to consider himself above "ordinary" people. He overestimated his own abilities and became angry when others did not recognize them. One of his most crushing defeats was in 1907, when he was seventeen and full of dreams about being an artist. Those dreams were dashed when he failed the entrance exam at the Academy of Fine Arts in Vienna. In his book, *Mein Kampf,* (My Struggle) Hitler described the disappointment:

> *I had set out with a pile of drawings, convinced that it would be child's play to pass the examination. At the [high school] I had been by far the best in my class at drawing, and since then my ability had developed amazingly; my own satisfaction caused me to take a joyful pride in hoping for the best. . . . Now I was in the fair city . . . waiting with burning impatience, but also with confident self-assurance, for the result of my entrance examination. I was so convinced that I would be successful that when I received my rejection, it struck me as a bolt from the blue. Yet that is what happened. When I presented myself to the rector, requesting an explanation for my non-acceptance . . . [he] assured me that the drawings I had submitted... showed my unfitness for painting . . .*[2]

Adolf Hitler as a young child. Of his mother's six children, only Adolf and his younger sister Paula survived to adulthood.

As a young man, Hitler had dreams of becoming an artist. He painted this watercolor in the early 1900s.

Primary Source—Hitler's Friend

When Adolf Hitler was impoverished and alone in Vienna, a young musician named August Kubizek befriended him. When the two became roommates, Kubizek often had difficulty coping with his friend's behavior:

> ***. . . In these early days in Vienna, I had the impression that Adolf had become unbalanced. He would fly into a temper at the slightest thing. There were days when nothing I could do seemed right to him and he made our life together very hard to bear . . . He was at odds with the world. Wherever he looked, he saw injustice, hate and enmity. Nothing was free from his criticism, nothing found favour in his eyes . . . Choking with his catalogue of hates, he would pour his fury over everything, against mankind in general who did not understand him, who did not appreciate him, and by whom he was persecuted.***[3]

Hitler came to hate Vienna. For him, it was a place of failure and poverty. Later in his life, he would recall how "foreign" the city had seemed to him: "I was repelled . . . by this whole mixture of [people:] Czechs, Poles, Hungarians, Ruthenians, Serbs and Croats . . . and everywhere . . . Jews and more Jews."[4] In the spring of 1912, Hitler left Austria and moved to Munich, Germany.

Fighting for Germany

Hitler was still in Munich two years later when Germany went to war. He quickly enlisted in the German army and marched off to fight for the Fatherland—the name Germans often used for their country. Though he never rose above the rank of corporal, Hitler found a place for himself in the army. In civilian life, he had been a shabby, failed artist with few friends and no social life. In the army he became somebody, at least in his own eyes.

The war gave Hitler an outlet for his fanatical German nationalism, or devotion to one's country. Hitler believed in "*Deutschland ueber Alles*," or "Germany over all." He believed that Germany should rule the world.

When Germany surrendered in 1918, Hitler's world fell apart. Defeat had been unthinkable. Only some dark and evil plot could explain it.

Looking for someone to blame, Hitler settled on Jews, Communists, and the new democratic government. Like other right-wing extremists in Germany, he concluded that a stab in the back from these traitors led to his country's defeat. This was not true, but for Hitler it was very real. In his rage, he decided to fight back by going into politics.

Hidden Talents

Hitler's road to political life began when the army recruited him to investigate radical, or extreme, political groups. One of his first assignments was to investigate a tiny political group called the German Workers' Party. On September 12, 1919, Hitler went to a meeting of about twenty-five people in a Munich beer hall.

He had only come to observe, but he couldn't resist speaking out. He shared his thoughts on German nationalism and pride. In the process, he demonstrated a talent for public speaking. His informal presentation stunned the audience, and left party founder Anton Drexler wide-eyed with admiration. He personally asked Hitler to return.

A few days later, Hitler received a postcard from the German Workers' Party. It said that he had been accepted as a party member. He was being invited to a meeting of the party leaders.

He did not know what to think. The party was little more than a debate group for people who didn't fit in elsewhere. Still, he could see advantages to joining "this absurd little organization with its few members. . . . Here it was still possible to work, and the smaller the movement, the more readily it could be put into the proper form."[5] In other words, he could become a leader almost immediately. In a larger, better-organized group he would never get that chance.

Hitler's speaking ability soon made him invaluable to the party. As one writer observed, "Even the earliest reports of Hitler as a speaker note the exchange of energy between him and his listeners. 'I had a peculiar sensation,' one eyewitness wrote in June 1919, 'as if their excitement was his doing and at the same time also gave him voice in return.'"[6]

Anton Drexler, the founder of the German Workers' Party, asked Hitler to join the organization after hearing him speak. The group would eventually become the Nazi Party.

The Party That Hitler Built

When Hitler's speeches began drawing new members, he convinced party leaders to organize larger meetings. He took it upon himself to promote those meetings by sending invitations, putting up flyers, and placing advertisements in nationalist and anti-Semitic newspapers. The crowds came, and listened to Hitler's speeches.

Success fed Hitler's desire for power. He pushed ahead, treating the party like modeling clay that he could shape and mold to his liking. Because his methods increased membership, the party leadership went along.

Rising Through the Ranks

Anton Drexler, founder of the party, was a plodding man with no talent for speaking or persuading people. He could, however, recognize these qualities in others. He saw them in Adolf Hitler.

With Drexler's support, Hitler rose quickly in the German Workers' Party. In January of 1920, he became chief of propaganda. His job was to spread the party's message.

Young Adolf Hitler quickly became a star in the German Workers' Party.

Hitler also worked with Drexler to write a party platform, or statement of goals and beliefs. It included removing Jews from government and newspaper jobs, renouncing the Treaty of Versailles, and creating a powerful government to control the life of the nation.

Hitler presented this platform at a party rally on February 24, 1920. Over two thousand people attended. Some came to see what the fuss was all about, some came to cheer, and some even came to heckle.

Hitler had a plan for the hecklers. A squad of his army friends went through the crowd with billy clubs and whips, clearing protestors from the hall. This security squad became the foundation for the dreaded Stormtroopers, or *Sturmabteilung* (SA).

Hitler's Street Fighters

The SA was organized by Ernst Röhm, a war veteran who was one of the earliest members of the party. Röhm was a battle-scarred bull of a man, ready to work with anyone who promised to make Germany strong again. Röhm believed he had found such a man in Hitler. Beyond that, he did not ask questions.

Röhm's Stormtroopers were street-fighters, always ready to crack heads, fight with rival groups, or terrorize anyone who criticized the party. They were often called Brownshirts because of the color of their uniforms. With their whips, clubs, and guns, they gave an image of toughness to the little party with the big ideas.

Hitler worked to strengthen that image. It was his idea to change the party name from the German Workers' Party to something more impressive: the National Socialist German

Ernst Röhm became the head of the Stormtroopers, who ruthlessly attacked anyone that posed a threat to the Nazi Party.

Primary Source—The Program of the German Workers' Party

In February 24, 1920, Hitler stood before a crowd of about two thousand and read the Program of the German Workers' Party. He and Anton Drexler had written it together. Though it reflected the party's nationalism and anti-Semitism, it was mostly a list of demands. Fifteen of the twenty-five clauses began with the words, "We demand." The clauses included:

1. *We demand the union of all Germans . . . on the basis of national self-determination.*
2. *We demand equality of rights for the German people in its dealings with other nations, and the revocation of the peace treaties of Versailles and Saint-Germain.*
4. *Only members of the nation may be citizens of the State. Only those of German blood . . . may be members of the nation. Accordingly, no Jew may be a member of the nation.*
8. *All non-German immigration must be prevented. We demand that all non-Germans who entered Germany after 2 August 1914 shall be required to leave the Reich forthwith.*
18. *We demand the ruthless prosecution of those whose activities are injurious to the common interest. Common criminals, usurers, profiteers, etc., must be punished with death, whatever their creed or race.*
22. *. . . To facilitate the creation of a German national press, we demand:*
    (a) *that all editors of, and contributors to, newspapers appearing in the German language must be members of the nation;*
    (b) *that no non-German newspapers may appear without the express permission of the State. They must not be printed in the German language;*
    (c) *that non-Germans shall be prohibited by law from participating financially in or influencing German newspapers, and that the penalty for contravening such a law shall be the suppression of any such newspaper, and the immediate deportation of the non-Germans involved.*[1]

Worker's (Nazi) Party. Nazi is an abbreviation of the first part of the German name: *Nationalsozialistische*.

Hitler also designed the party's flag, which would become a symbol of death and oppression to millions. He chose a red background with a black hooked "x," or swastika, inside a white circle. Soon, swastikas appeared everywhere at Nazi functions. They were on posters, banners, and flags. Swastika armbands decorated the khaki uniforms of the Stormtroopers.

A Convenient "Philosophy"

Behind the banners, uniforms, and rallies, was a political philosophy called Fascism. Fascism was the foundation of the Nazi party. The word comes from the name of an ancient Roman symbol of official authority. The fasces was a bundle of rods tied around two raised axe heads. The rods stood for punishment, the axe heads for execution. It was first used in 1919 to describe a political movement led by Benito Mussolini in Italy.

It is difficult to define Fascism. When Mussolini was asked for his definition, he simply replied, "It is action."[2] He did not like to be pinned down to a detailed ideology, or system of beliefs.

Hitler shared this attitude. Though he helped to write the Nazi platform, he did not feel bound by it. The party he wanted to build would not be based upon political philosophy. It would be held together by his leadership.

A Fascist leader is an absolute dictator whose word is law. Under his control, the State is not simply the nation's government. It is a total way of life. The State tells people how to behave, what to believe, and where to live and work. It even tells people how to raise and educate their children.

Dictator Benito Mussolini (seen here with Hitler) was the first Fascist leader in modern times. Hitler became an ally of Mussolini, although the two never fully trusted each other.

The idea of a constant struggle is important to Fascism. Among other things, fascists believe that constant struggle eliminates the weak and purifies the strong. In a fascist society, only the strong have a right to survive. This belief in the "survival of the fittest" makes fascist regimes brutal and warlike.

Fascists are also fiercely nationalistic, or patriotic to an extreme. They prefer conquest of other nations rather than cooperation. They fear any form of foreign influence.

In Nazi Fascism, only Germany mattered. Hitler made that clear in many writings and speeches. He explained his idea in simple words: "Our future is Germany. Our today is Germany. And our past is Germany. Let us take a vow this evening, at every hour, in each day, to think of Germany, of the nation, of our German people. You cannot be unfaithful to something that has given sense and meaning to your whole existence."[3]

Outmaneuvering the Opposition

This extreme nationalism appealed to the party leaders. Most of them agreed with the party platform outlined by Drexler and Hitler. Not all of them, however, liked Hitler as well as they liked his ideas. Many had become tired of his lectures and the tactics he used to get his way.

When a committee within the party tried to limit his growing power, Hitler moved swiftly to stop them. The way he handled the situation was masterful. It showed the sly cleverness that would serve him well in his rise to power. Instead of arguing his case, he simply offered to quit the party.

Primary Source—The Social Democratic Party Platform

The Social Democratic Party supported the Weimar Republic and its commitment to democracy. Its platform reflected those values:

We are committed to maintaining the Republic and a policy that will allow Germany to take its rightful place among the free governments of Europe.

1. *We will support the present German Republic so that freedom, democracy, and justice will live in the hearts of our German countrymen.*
2. *We will honor all of Germany's obligations, political and financial, in order that Germany's honor and respect will not be decreased in the eyes of the world.*
3. *We plan to create more jobs by creating an extensive program of public works.*
4. *We will provide unemployment compensation for up to six months.*
5. *We will cut government expenditures to lower taxes.*
6. *We believe in the right of those who disagree with the party to speak and write on those issues without interference.*[4]

The committee could not afford to lose Hitler. He was their best speaker and organizer. Without him, they would be back in dingy meeting rooms, doomed to insignificance.

When the committee refused to accept his resignation, Hitler knew he had the upper hand. He was quick to use it. He demanded total control of the party. There would be no more committee, no more bickering over details. There would only be his word, and his word would be law. After some frantic maneuvering on both sides, Adolf Hitler stood alone at the top of the Nazi party.

It was the beginning of the Führer Principle, establishing Hitler as Supreme Leader of the party. His every decision was law, and members swore undying loyalty to their Führer.

The Inner Circle

As Führer (leader) of the party, Hitler surrounded himself with loyal followers. Of the original party leaders, only Ernst Röhm kept a place of importance. Hitler felt a soldier's bond with Röhm. Both men had served in combat and shed blood for Germany.

Röhm's taste for violence served Hitler's purposes during the early days of his rise to power. Röhm's brute squad, the Stormtroopers, could always be counted on to keep order at meetings and rallies. Their presence was enough to silence most protest.

The rest of Hitler's inner circle was filled with men who idolized him. He did not want to surround himself with independent thinkers. He wanted people who would follow him blindly, yet were smart enough to know how to carry out his orders.

Early members of the inner circle included Rudolf Hess, Hermann Göring, and Heinrich Himmler. Each would later

Hitler and the *Munich Post*

In the early 1920s, the *Munich Post* newspaper began a twelve-year crusade against Hitler and his party. When Hitler first started, many people scoffed at his rabble-rousing. The journalists at the Post took him seriously. They criticized him, warned against the danger of his ideas, made fun of him.

Hitler hated the *Post,* claiming that it knowingly spread "poisonous" lies about him and about the Nazi party. Nothing he did could stop them. In 1923, during the Beer Hall *putsch,* or revolt he sent a detachment of Stormtroops to destroy the paper's offices and beat up anyone who happened to be there.

The *Munich Post* came back. It continued publishing attacks on the Nazis until March 1933, when then-Chancellor Adolf Hitler shut it down for good.

Egyptian-born Rudolf Hess was one of the very first members of the Nazi Party. He was known as a quiet man who was blindly loyal to Hitler.

play a leading role in the Third Reich. Each was a social misfit who shared Hitler's prejudices and hatreds. Each in his own way regarded the Führer with almost religious devotion.

The shy, hero-worshiping Hess was perhaps the most dedicated follower of all. As Hitler's personal aide he was always at the Führer's side. For Hess, this was enough. He did not crave power for himself. He was a born follower, content to live in Hitler's shadow and to obey every order.

Hermann Göring was far more ambitious. He was a decorated war veteran who shared Hitler's horror of the Treaty of Versailles. Raised among the aristocracy, or nobility, and trained in a military academy, Göring saw himself as a German hero. Peacetime had left him at loose ends. Göring found the cause he needed in the Nazi party.

He served in several different jobs. He was head of the SA for a time, and later became commander of the *Luftwaffe* (the German air force). Medals, awards, and impressive job titles fed his sense of self-importance.

Göring liked to think of himself as a man of action. He was not interested in the party's philosophy, or beliefs. He once said that he "joined the party because I was a revolutionary, not because of any ideological nonsense."[5]

Ideology, another word for beliefs, did interest Heinrich Himmler. A chicken farmer by trade, Himmler considered himself a mystic, a person interested in mysteries of life. He dabbled in astrology and other occult, or secret, practices. For him, belief in the German Master Race was practically a religion.

Many people found Himmler the most frightening of all the Nazi leaders. With his round, soft face and poor eyesight, he appeared to be the mildest of men. He did not rant like

Hermann Göring, a fighter pilot in World War I, earned Hitler's respect by bringing order to the Stormtroopers.

Hitler or strut like Göring. Yet he could unleash terror and mass murder without a pang of conscience.

Himmler became chief of Hitler's dreaded *Shutzstaffel*, or SS. This powerful organization combined security police and intelligence-gathering functions. Under Himmler's leadership, the SS would make Germany into a police state and be responsible for carrying out the Holocaust. As chief of the SS, Himmler could transform his darkest fantasies into even darker realities. He once called upon his troops to:

> be honest, decent, loyal and comradely to members of our own blood and to no one else. What happens to the Russians, what happens to the Czechs, is a matter of utter indifference to me. . . . Whether the other peoples live in comfort or perish of hunger interests me only in so far as we need them as slaves for our Kultur [culture].[6]

Hitler thoroughly approved of this harsh racism. For him, it was the heart and soul of Nazi ideology. He could not imagine that his Thousand-Year Reich would include Jews, people of color, or Slavs such as Poles and Russians. His empire would belong to a race of Aryan supermen. It would create *lebensraum*, or living space, for them by conquering vast territories in Eastern Europe and Russia.

"Nature . . . has not reserved this soil for the future possession of any particular nation or race," Hitler once wrote. "On the contrary, this soil exists for the people which possesses the force to take it."[7]

In Hitler's plan, Jews would be eliminated. Both Communism and democracy would be destroyed. In their place would be an all-powerful State, and a leader who could

Heinrich Himmler was placed in charge of the SS and would later be responsible for setting up the concentration camps under Hitler's supervision.

not be challenged or questioned by anyone. Hitler himself would be that leader for as long as he lived.

When Hitler first spoke of these things, few Germans took him seriously. He was just a "crackpot" with strange ideas and a handful of deeply disturbed followers. Not until the fall of 1923 did people begin to realize how far this "crackpot" would go to achieve his goals.

CHAPTER 3

Hitler's Revolt

Adolf Hitler lacked the patience to build the party bit by bit—a rally here, a speech there, a membership drive ever so often. He wanted to lead a bold strike against authority; something that would prove he had the makings of a heroic leader. He decided to stage a putsch, or revolt, against the Bavarian state government. (Bavaria is a German state.)

The idea was to capture government leaders and force them to surrender. Nazis would then seize the capital in Munich and transform the section of Germany known as "Bavaria" into a National Socialist state. Bavaria would then become a power base for spreading National Socialism throughout Germany.

A Small Revolution

Hitler was not the sort of man to bother with details. He often acted on impulse, without thinking his actions through. This led to mistakes. He would push too hard, then be surprised when things did not turn out the way he expected. This happened with what came to be called the Beer Hall putsch.

The public square in Munich, which was the site of the Beer Hall putsch of 1923.

Hitler's Revolt

On the night of November 8, 1923, Hitler burst into a Munich beer hall, where an important political meeting was in progress. Hess and Göring marched at Hitler's side. Ernst Röhm and his Stormtroopers sealed the exits.

Hitler fired his gun into the air. "The national revolution has broken out. The hall is surrounded," he shouted.[1]

Then Hitler herded Bavaria's three most important leaders into a back room. He threatened to shoot them if they did not give in to his demands: "Anyone who refuses to collaborate with me has no right to live. I have four bullets in my gun, three for [you] and the last for myself." He put the barrel to his temple: "If I am not victorious by tomorrow, I shall be a dead man."[2]

The men held their ground. Frustrated with their resistance, Hitler went back into the hall and began to speak to the crowd. Karl von Muller, who was at the meeting, later described that speech as a "masterpiece . . . In fact, in a few sentences, he totally transformed the mood of the audience. I have rarely experienced anything like it."[3]

The speech may have been impressive, but words alone could not carry the day. The captive officials still refused to cooperate. Hitler tried another tack, boasting that the war hero General Erich Ludendorff had agreed to command the armed forces of his new government.

Actually, Ludendorff had agreed to no such thing. He did not even know about the putsch. One of Hitler's men simply showed up at his doorway and asked him to come to the beer hall.

When Ludendorff arrived, he greeted the upstart corporal with a cold-eyed stare. But he did not leave. For reasons of his own, he decided to go along with the idea.

Hitler stands with two of his Brownshirts, or Stormtroopers, at the time of the 1923 Beer Hall putsch.

Under his influence, the three officials seemed to agree as well. Hitler was overjoyed, thinking he had won.

His happiness did not last for long. Later that night, the officials withdrew their support. None of them had joined the Nazis willingly, they said. They had been forced into making false statements.

Hitler was stunned. He was also furious. This reversal of fortune had caught him by surprise. Ludendorff suggested a simple, straightforward plan. He and Hitler, with all their followers, would march into the heart of the city and take over the War Ministry.

So it was that a legendary general and a former corporal led some three thousand Nazis into a battle they could not possibly win. The would-be revolutionaries never reached their goal. The police blocked their way.

There was an exchange of words, followed by an exchange of bullets that lasted only a minute. History does not record who fired the first shot. Sixteen Nazis and three policemen were killed. Many more people were wounded. The putsch came to a less than glorious end.

Going to Prison

Hitler and the Nazis appeared to be finished as a political force. Not only had they failed at their "revolution," they had looked foolish doing it. Under fire, Stormtroopers lost their swagger and scattered like frightened children. Hitler himself had run at the first sign of trouble. He took refuge in the home of friends, where he was arrested two days later.

If Hitler found his own behavior embarrassing or shameful, he gave no sign of it. In court, he relied on his famous speaking skills. He spoke well in his own defense, and people listened. In the end, the trial made Hitler into a national figure.

Some scoffed at him and his disorganized revolution. Others saw him, however misguided, as a patriot and hero. Even the judges were impressed. Many people were also sympathetic to his right-wing nationalism. They shared his dislike for the democratic constitution "forced" upon Germany after its defeat in World War I.

The judges could have sentenced Hitler to life in prison for high treason, or betraying the German nation. Instead, they sentenced him to five years. The other Nazi defendants also drew short prison terms, while General Ludendorff was found not guilty.

Hitler was sent to Landsberg Fortress, an old castle converted into a prison. Life at Landsberg was far from harsh. Hitler and his fellow revolutionaries had rooms instead of cells and were free to move about the prison's public areas.

While in prison, Hitler wrote his book, *Mein Kampf* (My Struggle). It was part autobiography, part political statement. It also served as a platform for Hitler's racist ideas. Rudolf Hess, imprisoned along with Hitler, helped edit, revise, and organize the material in *Mein Kampf*.

The Führer Returns

On December 20, 1924, Hitler was released from Landsberg, after serving less than a year of his sentence. He went into seclusion, staying with the family that had sheltered him after the failed putsch. Eventually, he started the long and difficult process of rebuilding the party.

It was not an easy job. After the putsch, the Bavarian government had outlawed the Nazi party. Some members

Hitler, seen here in his prison cell, received a five-year sentence for his role in the Beer Hall putsch.

Primary Source— The Putsch Trial: Hitler's Speech to the Court

After the Putsch trial ended, Hitler addressed the court. He did not admit wrongdoing. He praised himself and his motives and defied the Court:

> ***. . . The army which we have formed grows from day to day; it grows more rapidly from hour to hour. Even not I have the proud hope that one day the hour will come when these untrained... bands will grow to battalions, the battalions to regiments and the regiments to divisions, when the...old banners will once again wave before us and the reconciliation will come in that eternal last Court of Judgement... before which we are ready to take our stand... For, gentlemen, it is not you who pronounce judgment upon us it is the external Court of History which will make its pronouncement upon the charge which is brought against us. The verdict you will pass I know... You may pronounce us guilty a thousand times, but the Goddess who presides over the Eternal Court of History will with a smile tear in pieces the charge of the Public Prosecutor and the verdict of this court. For she aquits us.***[4]

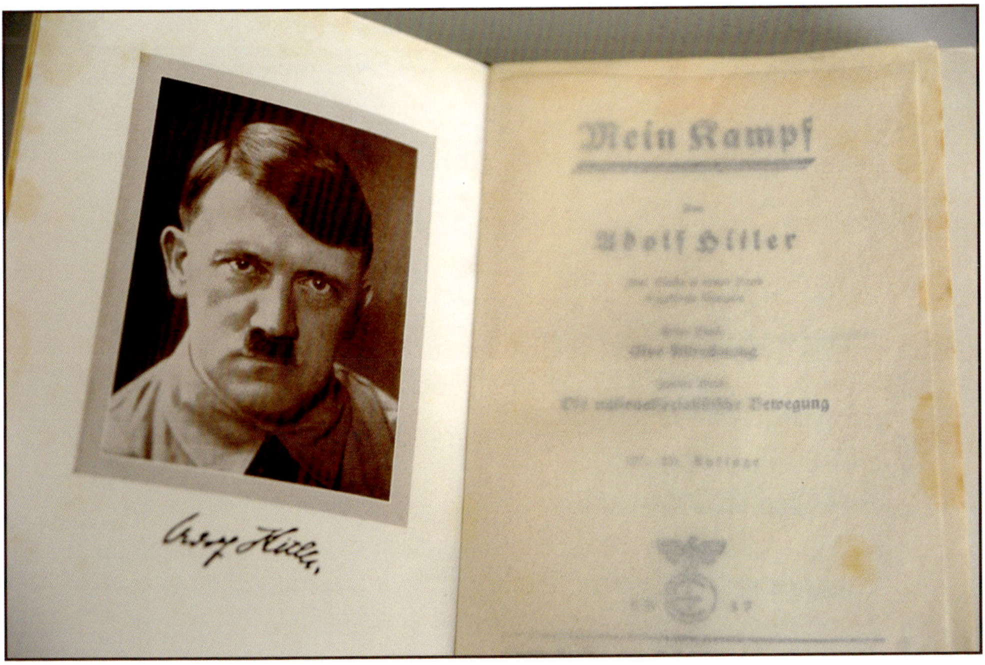

Mein Kampf (My Struggle) was an autobiographical treatise in which Hitler laid out his political views and described his vision of Germany's future.

Hitler's Prison Project

Prison life was far from hard for Adolf Hitler. He had a private room, good food, and facilities that included a library, a garden, and an open-air gym. Other prisoners used the facilities, gathered to talk or play cards. Hitler had other things on his mind. He wanted to set forth his master plan for the future of Germany and the world.

With the help of his devoted follower and secretary, Rudolf Hess, he wrote the book that came to be called *Mein Kampf*. His first title was *Four and a Half Years of Struggle Against Lies, Stupidity, and Cowardice*, but either Hess or his publisher talked him out of it.

went underground to keep it alive. Others formed organizations with new names so they could continue to play a public role.

Ernst Röhm replaced his banned Stormtroopers with a new private army called the *Frontbann*, or "Rulers of the Front." By the spring of 1925, he had mobilized over thirty thousand men.

Other Nazi party members formed a political organization called the National Socialist Freedom Movement. Its organizers included Alfred Rosenberg, the self-proclaimed philosopher of National Socialism. With the aid of General Ludendorff, Rosenberg's group entered candidates in the national elections of May 1925.

Thirty-four members of the National Socialist Freedom Movement ran for office. Thirty-two of them were elected. The successful candidates included General Ludendorff, Ernst Röhm, and a National Socialist organizer from Berlin named Gregor Strasser.

Adolf Hitler did not welcome this success. Though it brought National Socialism into the political mainstream, the success threatened his authority. That was a price the Führer was not willing to pay.

Yet another threat to his leadership came from a group centered around his old comrade, Anton Drexler. Drexler saw a chance to get even for past betrayals. He told anyone who would listen that Hitler had "[plotted] against me and broke all his promises, pushed me out, and now has wrecked the party for all time with this crazy Putsch!" Such a man would destroy the Nazi party if his power were not limited, Drexler said.

With all this opposition, even some Hitler loyalists wondered if their Führer could regain his former power.

Hitler is seen here leaving prison, just eight months after his sentencing. He was determined not to let the failure of the putsch derail his plans for the Nazis and Germany.

On February 27, 1925, he put their minds at rest. That night, he went back to the scene of the putsch to make his formal return to public life.

He was scheduled to speak at eight o'clock, but people began arriving in the afternoon. The hall was so crowded that more than a thousand people had to be turned away.

Inside the beer hall, there was barely room to stand. Four thousand people waited to hear Hitler. He spoke to them of party unity. He called upon them to stand together against Germany's greatest enemies: Communists and Jews.

By the time he finished speaking, the crowd was in a frenzy. People shouted "Heil Hitler!" The word *heil* (hail) refers to the act of greeting or acclaiming. The "Hitler salute" was not limited to rallies where the Führer appeared. It became part of everyday life. All over Germany and the occupied nations, loyal Nazis said hello and goodbye with a raised right hand and a hearty "Heil Hitler."

Running Afoul of the Government

Hitler's successful return to public life did not suit the Bavarian government. They banned the Nazi leader from speaking in public for two years. Bans in other German states soon followed. Gone were the giant rallies, the cheering crowds. Without them, Hitler could not hope to reach great masses of people. However, even the loss of his most powerful tool did not stop him.

During the ban, Hitler traveled across Bavaria, holding meetings with small groups of National Socialist Freedom Movement party members. He left the northern wing of the party in the hands of brothers Gregor and Otto Strasser in Berlin.

Primary Source—A Letter to Adolf Hitler, October 7, 1924

Houston Stewart Chamberlain was a British-born racist and "Aryan" supremacist. His ideas disgusted the English, but inspired Hitler. Chamberlain was equally inspired by the Nazi leader. A month before the Beer Hall putsch, he wrote what today might be called a "fan letter" to the future Führer:

Most respected and dear Herr Hitler:

You have every right to be surprised at this intrusion having seen with your own eyes how difficult it is for me to speak. But I cannot resist the urge to address a few words to you. I view this, however, as an entirely one-sided act, i.e. I do not expect an answer from you.

You are not at all, as you have been described to me, a fanatic. In fact, I would call you the complete opposite of a fanatic. The fanatic inflames the mind, you warm the heart. The fanatic wants to overwhelm people with words, you wish to convince, only to convince them—and that is why you are successful. Indeed, I would also describe you as the opposite of a politician, in the commonly accepted sense of the word, for the essence of all politics is membership of a party, whereas with you all parties disappear, consumed by the heat of your love for the fatherland. . . .

You have immense achievements ahead of you, but for all your strength of will I do not regard you as a violent man. You know Goethe's distinction between force and force. There is the force that stems from and in turn leads to chaos, and there is the force which shapes the universe. . . . It is this creative sense that I mean when I number you among the constructive men rather than those who are violent. . . .

My faith in Germandom has never wavered for a moment, though my hopes had, I confess, reached a low ebb. At one blow you have transformed the state of my soul. That Germany in its hour of greatest need has given birth to a Hitler is proof of vitality; your actions offer further evidence, for a man's personality and actions belong together. That the magnificent Ludendorff openly supports you and embraces your movement: what a wonderful combination! ... May God protect you![5]

Hitler did not like placing so much confidence in the Strassers, but he had no choice. Besides dealing with the ban, he had his hands full in Munich. His old friend and comrade Ernst Röhm was getting big ideas.

The *Frontbann* had been such a success that Röhm wanted to enlarge it. He dreamed of a vast private army, with himself in absolute control. To Hitler, that was unthinkable. He could not allow Röhm, or anyone else, to have such power.

The two leaders quarreled and, as usual, Hitler prevailed. Rather than accept a lesser role, Röhm quit the party and retired from politics. Hitler left the *Frontbann* to fend for itself. He had other matters on his mind, such as handling the Strasser brothers.

Dealing With the Opposition

The Strassers' views on what the party should become did not match Hitler's. They wanted to organize workers against big business. For Hitler, this was too close to Communist beliefs. He wanted to build a master race, not a nation of workers.

Hitler went to Berlin to deal with the problem personally. There, he met a man who would become one of the most important leaders in the Nazi empire. Joseph Goebbels did not fit the Nazi image at all. He was barely five feet tall, with dark eyes and olive skin. Childhood polio had left him with a crippled left foot and a noticeable limp.

During Hitler's time in Berlin, he won Goebbels to his side. In the long run, he was not as successful with the Strassers. However, he was able to silence them for a time with an appeal for party unity. This worked in part because the brothers were divided between themselves. Otto believed

Joseph Goebbels salutes Nazi soldiers. Goebbels worked closely with Hitler and successfully used propaganda to spread the Nazi message.

that Hitler was a danger to the party and to the German nation as a whole. Gregor considered him a figurehead who could be controlled. He was not the first, nor the last, person to make that mistake.

After settling the problem in Berlin, Hitler returned to Munich. On March 5, 1927, the Bavarian government lifted its public-speaking ban against him. The Führer promptly staged a mass meeting, complete with banners, music, marching troops, and a grand entrance.

Once more, Adolf Hitler had made a political comeback. This time, he would not make the mistake of starting a revolution he could not finish. This time, he had a plan. He would take over Germany without firing a shot or breaking a law.

Politics and Power

Adolf Hitler learned a hard lesson from the failure of his "revolution." In the late 1920s, he built a new image for himself. The wild-eyed revolutionary gave way to the impassioned defender of all things German. In public, he appeared more reasonable. People who had dismissed him as a hopeless rabble-rouser began listening to what he had to say.

Even with Hitler's new approach, the Nazi party did not control German politics. In fact, the democratic government seemed to be gaining ground. Germany was recovering from its postwar slump.

Hitler knew he needed a national disaster in order to grab power and transform Germany into what he wanted it to be. People did not listen to new and revolutionary ideas when times were good. They listened when times were bad, and the nation needed someone to lead it from the brink of disaster.

Bad Times at Last

From Hitler's point of view, the American stock market crash of October 1929, was a gift from the gods. Almost overnight,

Fair, slightly cooler tonight, Friday fair. Fresh southwest to west winds.

BROOKLYN DAILY EAGLE

And Complete Long Island News

LATE NEWS
WALL STREET 1:15 PRICES ★★

89th YEAR—No. 295. ★ NEW YORK CITY, THURSDAY, OCTOBER 24, 1929. ★ 32 PAGES THREE CENTS

WALL ST. IN PANIC AS STOCKS CRASH

Attempt Made to Kill Italy's Crown Prince

ASSASSIN CAUGHT IN BRUSSELS MOB; PRINCE UNHURT

Royal Suitor Was About to Lay Wreath on Unknown Soldiers' Tomb.

Princess, Deeply Moved, Falls Into Fiance's Arms and Kisses Him

Brussels, Oct. 24 (AP)—Crown Prince Humbert, after his return from the Unknown Soldier's Tomb where he escaped assassination, was receiving members of the Italian colony when his fiancee, Princess Marie Jose arrived. She hurriedly ran to him and fell in his arms, kissing him passionately. The pale complexion of the Princess indicated how deeply moved she was by the attempt on her fiance's life. The Prince said: "All's well that ends well and I have myself informed my mother that nothing happened to her son."

Brussels, Oct. 24 (AP)—A shot was fired at Crown Prince Humbert of Italy at 9:45 a.m. today as he was about to lay a wreath upon the tomb of Belgium's Unknown Soldier. The Prince arrived here yesterday to celebrate his betrothal to Princess Marie Jose of Belgium. The assassin was believed to be an Italian war veteran.

Hollywood Fire Destroys Films Worth Millions

ATTEMPT MADE ON LIFE

Crown Prince Humbert.

Consolidated Studios Are Swept by Flames Fatal to One—Master Pictures Burned Include Many New Talkie Productions.

Hollywood, Oct. 24 (AP)—One man was killed and motion picture films, the value of which probably will run into millions of dollars, were lost in an explosion and fire which destroyed the laboratory of the Consolidated Film Industries here early today.

Fifty persons working in the building at the time of the blast ran to safety after the first explosion. Five minutes later there was a second detonation which shot flames through windows and doors, the laboratory workers escaping by the narrowest of margins.

The body of Albert Lund was removd from th wrckag by firmen. He died on the way to a hospital.

Due to the fact that the master

Please Turn to Page 15

CARNEGIE CHARGE OF PAID ATHLETES ROUSES COLLEGES

HOOVER'S TRAIN HALTED BY AUTO PLACED ON RAILS

FEAR 52 PERISHED IN LAKE MICHIGAN; FERRY IS MISSING

Wreckage Picked Up Indicates Craft Went Down With All Aboard.

Milwaukee, Wis., Oct. 24 (AP)—Hope that the car ferry Milwaukee of the Grand Trunk fleet, with 52 aboard, had weathered the 48-hour storm on Lake Michigan faded today with a report that wreckage from a boat had been picked up 10 miles off Wind Point, which is about 4 miles north of Racine.

Capt. C. N. Bedell of the steamer Colonel told Grand Trunk officials here that he sighted empty lifeboats, mattresses and the upper parts of a white cabin, boating in the lake off Wind Point. The upper part of the Milwaukee was painted white.

Some of the wreckage was picked up by the Colonel, but not of it carried any markings to make identification certain, Captain Bedell said.

Freighter Donaldson Safe.

Superior, Wis., Oct. 24 (AP)—The freighter Donaldson, overdue here since Tuesday night, arrived this mornig from Apostle Islands, where it had put in to await abatement of the storm which swept the Great Lakes. The Donaldson was loaded with coal.

23 Rescued on Lake Huron.

Sault Ste. Marie, Mich., Oct. 24 (AP)—Twenty-three seamen and officers of the stranded steamer Maple Court of the Canada Steamship Lines were rescued by a Coast Guard cutter at 4:30 a.m. today from their vessel, which has been hard aground on Magnetic Reef, Cockburn Island, in Lake Huron, since 4 a.m. Sunday.

PIECE OF PLANE LIKE DITEMAN'S IS FOUND AT SEA

Black and Orange Wreckage Indicates Daring Flier Went to Death.

St. John's, N. F., Oct. 24 (by the Canadian Press)—The report from Harbor Grace that the S.S. Kyle had picked up a message from an unidentified ship concerning the finding of airplane wreckage was stated by the Newfoundland management to be without foundation. the management has had no message from the Kyle.

Harbor Grace, N. F., Oct. 24 (AP)—A radio message from "Operator Serrick" of the S. S. Kyle today advised that he had picked up a Marconi message from the S. S. Scythia that another ship, name unknown, had discovered a piece of airplane wreckage at 2 p.m. yesterday. The wreckage was black and orange. The message did not give the ship's position.

The S.S. Kyle is presumably the Newfoundland Government ship of that name.

[The little plane in which Urban F. Diteman essayed to cross the Atlantic from Harbor Grace to London had a black fuselage and its wings were painted orange.]

No Diteman Gas in Greenland.

Copenhagen, Oct. 24 (AP)—Daugaard Jensen, Governor of Greenland, today informed the Associated Press that the Greenland trade never had heard from Urban Diteman, missing flier, and that no gasoline depots had been laid

High Duty Group Gave $700,000 to Coolidge Drive

Grundy Agrees Rates Went Up Due to His Activities as Propagandist. Favors More Lobbying to 'Carry Out Voters' Wish.'

Eagle Bureau, Capitol Bldg.

By HENRY SUYDAM.

Washington, Oct. 24—Joseph R. Grundy, Bristol, Pa., manufacturer who admittedly has been lobbying in the capital for several decades in the interest of a protective tariff, testified before the Senate Lobby Committee today that he raised $700,000 for President Coolidge's campaign in 1924 and that most of the money came from interests seeking higher tariffs.

He intimated that he was in favor of more lobbying for higher du-

Please Turn to Page 2.

FOR MORE LOBBYISTS

JOSEPH R. GRUNDY

WARDER SOUGHT TO KEEP SEA TRIP SECRET, AID SAYS

SOMERS NAMED AS HEAD OF NEW EXCHANGE BANK

STOCKS CRASH IN RUSH TO SELL; BILLIONS LOST

Morgan, Mitchell Buying Stocks in Effort to Check Rush to Unload.

Wall Street was in a panic today, with no one to guide it out. Stocks crashed 10 to 50 points to outrageous levels. Wheat broke 10 cents a bushel in Chicago on distress selling. Bankers were offering some support, but admitted the situation had gotten beyond them.

Charles E. Mitchell, chairman of the National City Bank, was conferring in the office of J. P. Morgan & Co., it was understood, and other leading bankers were there.

It was also understood the Morgan partners had been talking by telephone with J. P. Morgan in London all morning.

By noonday the best information was that they had been buying stocks, but that the situation had gotten beyond them.

Panic reigned on the Stock Exchange today. Stocks broke terrifically, without any support whatever. Declines of 10 and 20 points were widespread. Selling was at a furious pace. There were few buyers. Five million shares were sold in two hours.

The headlines of a New York newspaper announce the stock market crash of 1929. Hitler took advantage of the worldwide panic to unite Germans behind him.

rich people lost their fortunes and ordinary people, their life savings. As the American crisis grew, it affected economies all over the world.

In Germany, thousands were thrown out of work. Hopes for prosperity vanished. Communist activity increased, to the great fear of the average German in the middle class. Hitler played the situation with a sure hand. A vast conspiracy of Communists and Jews was responsible for Germany's woes, he said. Unless someone stopped them, they would destroy the German Fatherland.

In speeches all over Germany, Hitler presented himself as that someone. People who had mocked him before began to listen. Nazi party membership grew. So did Nazi presence in the German government. In the election of 1930, Nazi representation in the *Reichstag*, or parliament, shot up from twelve seats to 107.

The Old Guard and the New Ways

Hitler's new image as "savior" of the Fatherland may have appealed to the German middle class, but it did not appeal to the SA. After the ban on the Nazi party was lifted, the Brownshirts had come back in force. They were still street brawlers at heart. To them, Hitler's campaigning was a sign of weakness.

The new leader of the SA, Franz Pfeffer von Salomon, wanted to turn the SA into a powerful army. His idea was simple: Forget politics and persuasion. Take control by force.

Hitler wanted the SA to be more disciplined, and he insisted that it be under his personal control. Salomon resigned because of his disagreements with the Führer.

In desperation, Hitler recalled Röhm from retirement. The Führer named his old comrade to head the SA again.

He promised not to interfere in SA matters. In return, he expected the SA to swear an oath of allegiance to him.

Röhm agreed to Hitler's terms. In less than four years Rohm helped it grow from 70,000 to 4.5 million members.[1] Many members were not former soldiers, but criminals with a violent past.

Under Röhm, the Brownshirts became terrorists, crushing anyone who opposed the Party or its Führer. SA units harassed Jews, Communists, and anyone else whose loyalty to Nazism was questionable.

Because the SA was not officially an arm of the Nazi party, Hitler did not have to take responsibility for its actions. While the Brownshirts cracked heads, he could continue passing himself off as a statesman. As he gained confidence in the political arena, he moved more surely toward his goal of gaining absolute power.

Hitler's First Election

In 1932 the former corporal from Austria ran for president of Germany. Hitler's opponent was the current president, Paul von Hindenburg. The aristocratic Hindenburg held the rank of field marshal, highest in the German military. As commander of the army during World War I, he had become a living legend. He first won the presidency in 1925, at the age of seventy-eight.

Hindenburg ran again in 1932, at the advanced age of eighty-five. His only real opposition in that election was Adolf Hitler. Hitler did not run for president because he wanted the office, or even because he thought he could win. He ran because the Nazi party needed a candidate, and he needed the stage a national election would give him.

Members of the SA march past Hitler in Nuremburg, Germany. The Brownshirts, as they were known, were used to intimidate and often terrorize anyone who opposed the Nazis.

He did not win the election. However, he did force a runoff—a vote to choose between the two candidates. In that second election, he won 36.1 percent of the vote. That was a good showing against a national hero. It served notice to the German public that Hitler and the Nazis had come to stay. It also paved the way for Hitler's real goal of becoming chancellor of Germany.

A Foot in the Door

In a parliamentary government, the chancellor, or chief of state, is appointed by the president. His first task is to put together a governing majority in the parliament, or legislature. In a system with several political parties, that is often a difficult thing to do. The chancellor must convince two or more parties to work together. If he fails, the president can dissolve the parliament and call for new elections.

This happened twice during 1932. In the first election that July, the Nazis won 230 of approximately 550 seats in the Reichstag. The second election was held in November. But four months had made a big difference in public attitudes. The German people had grown impatient with their stumbling economy. They voted many representatives out of office.

The Nazis lost thirty-four Reichstag seats in the November election. This was a hard blow. The two election campaigns had left the party nearly broke. Some members quit after this reversal of fortune. Others simply stopped paying their party dues.

In such a crisis, most politicians would become cautious. Adolf Hitler did not. He openly sought the chancellorship. To get it, he used the same tactics that had once swept Anton Drexler and others out of his way.

Hitler made an all-or-nothing gamble. He would become chancellor in return for Nazi cooperation in a new government. He flatly refused any lesser position. Some of Hitler's closest advisors disagreed with this tactic. They wanted him to consider a cabinet minister's post or some other important position. Either would give the Nazis a good foundation in national politics. The rest could come later.

The Führer considered this approach timid and unworthy. He held firm: the chancellorship or nothing. The situation looked hopeless for the Nazis until help came from an unexpected source.

Former Chancellor Franz von Papen threw his support behind Adolf Hitler. Papen himself had been unable to form a government by uniting the nationalist, anti-democratic parties. He believed that the Nazi leader could succeed where he had failed.

The chief obstacle to a Hitler chancellorship was President von Hindenburg. The old field marshal was an aristocrat and supporter of royalty. He did not like Hitler, who "did not come from the right social class and had only been a corporal in the war."[2]

Papen knew he faced a difficult task when he sat out to change von Hindenburg's mind. He met with the would-be chancellor in January 1933, to work out acceptable terms. Then he approached von Hindenburg, arguing that Hitler would be chancellor in name only. Hitler could be controlled, he said. Papen himself would become vice-chancellor. He would run the government while "the corporal" became little more than a figurehead, a front man without real power. On these terms, the president finally agreed.[3]

Franz von Papen, seen here in 1932, convinced President von Hindenburg to appoint Hitler to the chancellorship. He wrongly believed that Hitler could be controlled once he was in office.

Primary Source—Hitler Comes to Power

The *Manchester Guardian*, January 31, 1933:

Hitler's long-cherished ambition to become Chancellor has at last been satisfied. President von Hindenburg appointed him Chancellor of the Reich at noon today—an hour which may prove a turning-point in the history of post-war Germany, and which at any rate marks another victory for the reactionary forces. . . .

The news of Hitler's appointment created a feeling of alarm and confusion almost everywhere. To the average German it marks a leap in the dark. Even many Conservatives completely in sympathy with the [Nationalists] have been shaking their heads. . . .

The rank-and-file Socialists . . . are feeling bitterly on the subject and . . . are speaking. . . of the need of a "united front" with the Communists—which to their mind is the only way to salvation. . . .

The Nazis, of course, are jubilant, and the prospect that the storm detachments may now be incorporated in the State apparatus appeals to them enormously. In the meantime they expect to receive financial support from Hitler's wealthy Cabinet colleagues.

Hitler's supporters, many of them wearing the Nazi uniform, were even rowdier and more pugnacious than usual when they crowded outside the Kaiserhof this afternoon to welcome their leader, the new Chancellor.

When at last Hitler, dressed in a brown tweed suit and looking pale and more self-conscious than ever, came out of the hotel and drove off in his car the enthusiasm of the crowd outside was wild.[4]

Chancellor Hitler

On January 30, 1933, Adolf Hitler became chancellor of Germany. As he had vowed after his release from Landsberg Prison, he came to power legally. Not a shot was fired; not a law was broken. The new chancellor soon proved that he would not be just a figurehead. He also proved that even the second highest position in the government would not satisfy him. With each step along the road to power, Adolf Hitler wanted more.

He moved quickly to get it. He knew that the best way to unify people was to give them a common enemy. He had already chosen that enemy: the Communists.

Just one day after becoming Chancellor, Hitler held a conference with Hermann Göring and Joseph Goebbels. The three men developed a plan that began with Göring giving police powers to fifty thousand Stormtroopers. Two days later, the new "policemen" raided Communist headquarters in Berlin.

Göring claimed that the raid had uncovered plans for a Communist uprising. Actually, Göring's men found the membership list of the Party, and he planned to arrest all its members.

The Reichstag Fire

On February 27, 1933, fire raged through the Reichstag building, and the "Communist threat" became the talk of Berlin. Communist sympathizer Marinus van der Lubbe was arrested at the scene. He had a history of mental problems and a police record for starting fires in public buildings around Berlin.

A crowd swarms Hitler as he leaves his hotel to lead his first cabinet session as chancellor.

Van der Lubbe may have set a small blaze, but the main fire was almost certainly the work of the SA. Historians are not quite sure how van der Lubbe became involved. Most likely, the Nazis tricked him into starting a fire. At any rate, he was on hand to take the blame.

The Nazis claimed that this was the beginning of a Communist attempt to overthrow the lawful government of Germany. Herman Göring stirred up public fear with talk of Communist "terror squads" waiting to launch civil war. He said that they had "organized to poison food . . . and burn down granaries [storage units for harvested grain] . . . They planned to use every kind of weapon—even hot water, knives and forks and boiling oil!"[5]

While Göring dealt with the public, Hitler convinced Hindenburg that the danger was real. On the day after the fire, the president signed an emergency decree, or order. It suspended individual rights such as freedom of speech and assembly, and allowed police to make searches without warrants. It gave the chancellor broad powers to act against enemies of the state.

The Nazis continued to whip up public hysteria about the "Red Menace," as they called the Communists. They hoped to turn those fears into a landslide victory in the next Reichstag election. They did not, however, entirely achieve that goal.

The Nazis and their allies won a small majority of seats in the Reichstag, but not the sweeping victory they wanted. In what was to be the last free election until after World War II, the Germans gave the Nazis 44 percent of the vote.

Primary Source—Minutes of the Conference of Ministers on March 7, 1933

Marinus van der Lubbe was arrested on February 27, 1933. Eight days later, officials met to discuss his fate. The law said he should go to prison, but the ministers did not mind breaking the law to serve their purposes. Marinus van der Lubbe was found guilty on December 23, 1933. Less than a month later, he was beheaded.

The Reich Minister of the Interior . . . spoke about the Reichstag fire and the punishment of the culprits, and stated that it was urgently necessary to hang van der Lubbe at once. . . . the law that currently applied to arson only provided for a prison sentence, but it had to be possible to impose the penalty of death by hanging for such a heinous crime and to apply it retroactively. . . .

The Chancellor stressed the fact that, in his opinion also, it was urgently necessary to hang van der Lubbe. The German public absolutely expected this. He could not recognize the doctrine of "the law must be observed," if the entire national life had to perish as a result. . . . State Secretary Dr. Schlegelberger stated that he agreed entirely with the view of the Reich Chancellor that the law had to be adjusted to the circumstances.

A preliminary investigation of van der Lubbe had opened today (March 7) on grounds of high treason and arson. . . .

State Secretary Dr. Meissner said that the statements of the Chancellor were entirely correct from a political perspective. The public was right in demanding a severe punishment for van der Lubbe. . . .

The Reich President [Hindenburg], however, might twice suffer severe qualms of conscience, namely, if he were to sign an order prescribing the death penalty, etc., and then again if he were to decide later on to pardon the condemned man. He asked that the Reich Chancellor, the Reich Minister of the Interior, and the Reich Minister of Justice [Gürtner] submit the matter to the President before there was a final decision by the Cabinet. . . .

It was expected that the Chancellor would first speak alone with the President concerning the matter.[6]

Marinus van der Lubbe stands trial for the Reichstag fire in 1933. He was found guilty and condemned to death.

Climbing Upward

Despite this disappointment, Hitler moved ahead with the next step in his climb to power. His plan was to get the Reichstag to give him its power to make laws. To do this, he once more used the threat of a Communist takeover. The Reds were planning to take over Germany, he said. In order to stop them, he needed the power to move quickly. The Enabling Law, as it was called, would give him that power.

This law involved changing the German constitution. It required the support of a two-thirds majority in the Reichstag. When the Nazis could not put together enough votes to get that majority, Hitler fell back on an old habit. He played the statesman while the SA behaved like street rowdies.

On the day the Reichstag was supposed to vote on the Enabling Law, the SA turned out in force. They prevented Communist delegates from entering the Reichstag to vote. Hitler gained the majority he needed.

The Enabling Law gave Hitler powers as a dictator. He could make new laws without consulting the Reichstag or the president. He could even violate the constitution if he thought it was necessary.

Hitler moved swiftly to consolidate his position. One of his first acts was to order a nationwide boycott of Jewish businesses for April 1. People would not do business with Jews on this day. He followed this with a law that excluded Jews from all government jobs.

On July 14, 1933, he proclaimed the Nazi party the only legal political party in Germany. All others either disbanded voluntarily or were shut down by the SA.

There were only two things left in Hitler's way: President Hindenburg and the Army High Command. The old field marshal was already fading. Hitler was content to play a waiting game with him. He could not do the same with the army, though. He would need the support of the High Command to build a solid base of power. In order to get that support he would have to control Ernst Röhm and the SA.

Cleaning Up Loose Ends

It was becoming clear that Röhm had outlived his usefulness. By 1933 the SA had more than two million members. It was a danger to the regular army and also the Nazi party. To make matters worse, Röhm became involved in a homosexual scandal that made the front page of the Munich newspaper. The Führer made a great show of being shocked to discover that the SA harbored homosexuals and violent criminals.

Something had to be done, he said. He called on Heinrich Himmler and Hermann Göring to handle the problem. By this time, Himmler had built the SS into a disciplined and fanatical force loyal to Hitler. Göring had formed the Gestapo, an equally fearsome secret police unit in the German state of Prussia.

On June 30, 1934, the SS and Gestapo began a purge of the SA. It came to be known as "the Night of Long Knives," though the killing lasted for more than three days. Dozens of Brownshirts and others suspected of disloyalty were imprisoned or killed outright. Others, including Röhm himself, were arrested and later executed.

According to reports from witnesses, the SS executioners gave Röhm a loaded gun. This was to allow him the "honorable" alternative of suicide. Röhm did not use the gun. "If I am to be killed, let Adolf do it himself," he said.[7]

A sign announced the boycott of Jewish businesses shortly after Hitler took power in 1933.

"Swift as a Greyhound, as Tough as Leather, and as Hard as Krupp's Steel"

This phrase summed up Hitler's goal for young Germans. He first used it in public at a Nazi Party rally in 1935. It went on to become a slogan of the Hitler Youth movement. Toughness alone was not enough. The Hitler Youth were also indoctrinated with racism, anti-Semitism, and fanatical loyalty to Germany and to the Führer.

The youth program had much in common with military basic training. Boys learned close-order drill and how to handle firearms. There were also groups for younger boys and for girls. In 1939 membership in one of these programs became compulsory for all young people.

Germans were taught to be loyal to the Nazi Party at a very young age. When they turned ten, the children were expected to join the Hitler Youth organization. There were separate groups for girls and boys.

Then he stood at attention until the executioners shot him dead.

Among the victims of the Night of Long Knives was Hitler's rival Gregor Strasser. The man who had wanted a truly socialist state was gunned down in his jail cell. Otto Strasser managed to escape his brother's fate. He left the country and eventually found his way to Canada.

The Night of Long Knives changed the Nazi party. The SA was in shambles and its leaders were dead. Hitler was finally able to win army support. All he had to do now was wait until the ailing Hindenburg was out of the way.

Karl Ernst was an SA leader who was among those killed on the Night of the Long Knives.

CHAPTER 5

The Führer's War

Hitler did not have long to wait for long. Von Hindenburg died on August 2, 1934. By this time, Hitler did exactly what he needed to do; paid public tribute to the fallen hero, and accepted the "burden" that fell on his shoulders with a show of humility. Then he promptly combined the offices of president and chancellor and proclaimed himself Supreme Leader of the German Nation.

The new Führer set to work, recasting Germany into a police state, and bringing Nazism to the masses. He envisioned a Reich, or empire, that would last a thousand years. It would push aside "lesser" peoples and ensure the dominance of the "master race."

Creating the Reich

The SS played a major role in making Germany into a Nazi state. Under the sinister Heinrich Himmler, the SS had become a vast monster. Many parts had overlapping authority. Criminal police dealt with ordinary crimes, such as burglary and assault. State security police dealt with

Hitler speaks at President von Hindenburg's funeral in 1934. Upon the president's death, Hitler declared that the titles of chancellor and president would be combined. In doing so, he removed all checks and balances to his power and became absolute ruler.

Primary Source—Hitler Pays Tribute to Hindenburg

Hitler gave a moving speech at Hindenburg's funeral. He sounded entirely sincere. Yet as soon as the President died, he rushed to issue a decree that made him absolute ruler of the German nation:

Herr und Frau von Hindenburg! Esteemed Mourners! Generals, Officers and Soldiers of the Wehrmacht!

A soldier is normally honored twice in his life: following a victory and following his death... When the German Volk first received word of the name of General Paul von Hindenburg, the tempests of the World War were raging over Europe. In the worst hours, the Kaiser recalled the General from retirement and assigned him the command of the Army in East Prussia. And six days later, the cannons were booming . . . three days [after that] ... the battle of Tannenberg had been won. . . .

And when—unfortunately too late—the Kaiser appointed him to head the entire Army, he was able ... to banish the most severe crisis for the time being. . . .

The tragic end of that great struggle cannot be held against this commander in history, but is instead a condemnation of the politicians . . .

Nearly twenty years ago today, the bells sounded here and echoed throughout Germany ... in honor of the name of the Field Marshal. Today, to the peal of these same bells, the nation has accompanied its ... departed hero back to the great battlefield of his unequaled victory. It is here, in the midst of the slumbering grenadiers of his victorious regiments, that the tired commander shall find his rest. . . .

Dead Commander, enter into Valhalla now![1]

racial issues, ensured loyalty to the Führer, and punished those who would not go along. Even Hermann Göring's Gestapo became part of the SS.

The SS and the Gestapo turned Germany into a brutal National Socialist society. There was National Socialist education, law, medicine, commerce, and industry. There was even National Socialist recreation and entertainment.

All loyal Germans were expected to belong to one or more Nazi groups. Young people joined the Hitler Youth. Adults had a dizzying variety of professional associations, sports clubs, and social groups. Membership in these groups was not voluntary. Everybody had to belong and everybody had to attend. Those who did not could expect an unpleasant visit from the SS or Gestapo.

Most importantly, every German was expected to show proper reverence for the Führer. Criticism was not allowed. Neither was joking at the Führer's expense. Hitler became a godlike figure, for even his closest associates.

This "Führer Principle," as it came to be called, became the center of public life. People greeted one another with "Heil Hitler," raising their right arms in salute. Propaganda chief Joseph Goebbels summed up the supposed power of Adolf Hitler in a few brief sentences:

> He alone is never mistaken. He is always right. Amazing how great the Führer is in his simplicity and how simple his greatness. He is above us all. He is always like a great star above us.[2]

Sebastian Haffner, a German lawyer and opponent of Hitler, wrote about living in the Nazi state: ". . . the state demands that the individual give up his friends . . . renounce

Germans showed their loyalty to Hitler with the right-hand salute and a "Heil Hitler!"

his beliefs, and assume new [approved] ones. He must use a new form of greeting, eat and drink in ways he does not [like], employ his leisure in occupations he [despises], and deny his past and his individuality. For all this, he must constantly express extreme enthusiasm and gratitude."[3]

Racial "Science"

In addition to a proper attitude toward National Socialism, Germans were expected to be conscious of race. Only people of German and Northern European heritage were to be part of the Nazi future. Jews, people of color, and other non-Aryans did not belong. Their very blood was thought to be polluted, or dirty.

Even full Aryans were not entirely safe from Nazi racial policies. One of the earliest laws was aimed at Germans with genetic, or inherited, diseases. The Law for the Prevention of Genetically Diseased Offspring became official on July 14, 1933. It allowed forced sterilization of people with hereditary diseases. By preventing these people from having children, the Nazis hoped to improve the so-called Aryan race.

On the other side of the coin, the Nazis called upon genetically healthy Aryans to produce as many children as possible. The responsibility for this fell chiefly upon women. German women were told to bear children early and often. They were told that this was the purpose of their existence.

Controlling reproduction was an important part of the Nazi racial hygiene movement. The word *hygiene* simply means the promotion and preservation of health. There is nothing sinister, or evil, about it. Racial hygiene is another matter. The Nazis used it to serve their notion of a German master race.

Hitler encouraged "pure" German women to have many children in order to continue the Aryan race. Here, Minister of Propaganda Goebbels poses with his wife and children.

In the name of racial hygiene, the Nazis prohibited intermarriage between Aryans and non-Aryans. An Aryan who married or partnered with a Jew or person of color was a race criminal and could go to prison. Children of these unions were mongrels.

In time, the myth of the master race would take Germany beyond controlling who had children and who did not. It would be used to justify the killing of "defective" babies and mentally ill children and adults. It would furnish a reason for genocide, the systematic killing of entire peoples.

Spreading the Empire

Nazi racial policies were linked to plans for expanding German territory. Hitler wanted *lebensraum*, or living space, for all those large, Aryan families. He intended to get it by any means necessary, including war.

Before he could carry out his plan for German expansion, Hitler had to rebuild the military, a process called rearmament. He started in secret, building Germany's military strength while continuing to declare his peaceful intentions.

On March 16, 1933, Hitler went public, announcing that he would begin military conscription (the draft), increasing the army to 550,000 men.[4] The Treaty of Versailles was broken, but the nations of Europe did not respond.

A year later, the new German army marched into the Rhineland (an area in western Germany). Hitler was quick to point out that this was not an invasion. The troops entered peacefully. No shots were fired, no blood was spilled. The army was simply protecting the interests of Rhineland Germans.

With each step, Hitler grew bolder. In March 1938, Germany took over Austria; again, without war. He browbeat and threatened Austrian leaders into holding a special election. Voters approved the *anschluss*, or annexation, of Austria to the German Reich.

Next, Hitler went after Czechoslovakia. First came the Sudentenland, a region along the Czech-German border. Once again, there was no bloodshed. Hitler took the territory with the unwitting help of British Prime Minister Neville Chamberlain.

In the Munich Agreement of October 4, 1938, Chamberlain agreed not to oppose Hitler's move on the Sudentenland. In return, Hitler promised that he would make no more territorial demands in Europe.

Chamberlain thought he had made "peace for our time." A newsreel of his return to England shows him waving the agreement before cheering crowds, and calling it "symbolic of the desire of our two peoples never to go to war with one another again."[5]

Just six months later, Germany took all of Czechoslovakia. Once again, there was no bloodshed. The Nazis intimidated the Czech leadership and maneuvered them into accepting the new order. England and the other Versailles powers did nothing.

And Then Came War

When Hitler started making demands on Poland, England and France stepped in to guarantee Polish borders. Hitler ignored them. He signed a nonaggression pact with Josef Stalin, to keep the Soviet Union out of his way, and he was ready.

Prime Minister Neville Chamberlain arrives back in England after signing an agreement with Hitler that he thought would ensure peace. The mistake ultimately cost him his career.

Primary Source—London: BBC Report: September 1, 1939

GERMANY INVADES POLAND

German forces have invaded Poland and its planes have bombed Polish cities, including the capital, Warsaw:

The attack comes without any warning or declaration of war.

Britain and France have mobilized their forces and are preparing to wage war on Germany for the second time this century.

Just before dawn today, German tanks, infantry and cavalry penetrated Polish territory on several fronts with five armies, a total of 1.5 million troops.

Soon afterward, German planes bombarded the cities. They have been making swift progress in penetrating Polish defences which are heavily outnumbered in artillery, infantry and air power.

The cities of Katowice, Krakow, Tczew, and Tunel were attacked with incendiary bombs. Air raids on Warsaw began at 0900 local time.

Communications with Katowice have been broken but earlier reports said German planes were coming over in squadrons of 50, every half hour, and there have been many casualties.

The German army struck from Slovakia East Prussia, and from Pomerania into the Polish corridor and the port [of] Danzig, which had declared itself part of the Reich.

The 4th army came in from East Prussia supported by air raids on cities north of Warsaw. There is heavy fighting reported along the whole of the East Prussian border.

Poznan was attacked from the main body of the German Reich and border towns occupied.

The 8th and 10th armies are moving north-east from Silesia; towards Warsaw; and the 14th army struck from Slovakia towards Krakow. . . .

The unprovoked attack follows yesterday's report on German radio that the border town of Gliwice had been raided by a group of Polish soldiers, who had all been shot dead.[6]

On September 1, 1939, Nazi troops invaded Poland. Two days later, Britain and France declared war on Germany. One of the darkest chapters in human history had begun.

The Legacy Continues

World War II ended in Europe on May 8, 1945. Allied troops had marched from the beaches of France to the heart of Germany. Along the way, they liberated Nazi concentration camps, and what they found shocked the world.

Everywhere it was the same; prisoners in the last stage of starvation, dead bodies scattered over the grounds or thrown into piles. American General George S. Patton was known for his toughness. On the battlefield, nothing fazed him, but his first visit to a camp left him shaken. He called it "one of the most appalling sights I have ever seen."[7]

Over time, the world learned more about the Nazi campaign against the Jews. Each new fact seemed more chilling than the one before it. Survivors and others kept the memories alive, as a tribute to the six million Jews who died, and as a warning about the terrible cost of hatred. "Never forget" became the motto of Holocaust remembrance.

In the twentieth century, the Holocaust was remembered in many ways. Survivors told their stories in meeting halls and classrooms. Governments and private foundations built Holocaust museums and memorials. They collected the testimonies of survivors, liberators, and others into vast archives. The nation of Israel created a "Holocaust Remembrance Day" that was observed in many countries.

In the twenty-first century, "Never forget" remains the motto, but time has brought changes. The Holocaust is passing from living memory into history. Jonathan Sacerdoti, of the Campaign Against Anti-Semitism, spoke

The Fate of Neville Chamberlain

With the invasion of Poland, British Prime Minister Neville Chamberlain's hopes for "peace in our time" collapsed. On September 3, 1939, he faced a dreaded task: making a formal declaration of war on Germany.

The man who had been cheered when he brought home the Munich Agreement found himself in political disgrace. He had made the mistake of taking Hitler at his word. His policy of appeasement had failed. In spite of a long career in public service, he would be forever remembered for that one mistake.

He did not remain in office for long. On May 10, 1940, he resigned as Prime Minister, and Winston Churchill took his place. Chamberlain remained as a member of Churchill's cabinet until his health forced him to retire. He moved to the country, where he died of cancer on November 9, 1940.

A concentration camp survivor, wearing his prisoner number, attends the seventieth anniversary commemoration of the liberation of the Sachsenhausen concentration camp.

about honoring that history: "It is more important than ever that we commemorate the Holocaust as we begin to enter an era when commemorations will have to be done by those who weren't there themselves."[8]

Why is commemoration still so important? There are many reasons: social, moral, and political. For Roman Kent, an eighty-five-year-old Auschwitz survivor, the answer was simple: "We survivors do not want our past to be our children's future."[9]

TIMELINE

1918—End of World War I. Germany surrenders.

1919—Treaty of Versailles is signed. Germany is forced to accept strict terms. Adolf Hitler attends his first meeting of the German Workers' Party.

1920—German Workers' Party becomes the National Socialist German Workers' (Nazi) Party.

1923—Beer Hall putsch takes place.

1924—Hitler is sentenced to five years in prison for the putsch; he is released from Landsberg Prison after serving less than nine months of his sentence.

1925—Bavarian government bans Hitler from public speaking.
Ernst Röhm withdraws from public life. Hitler creates the SS.

1927—Bavarian government lifts the speaking ban on Adolf Hitler.

1933—**January 30:** Hitler is sworn in as chancellor of Germany.

February 27: Reichstag fire occurs.

February 28: Presidential decree grants Hitler emergency powers.

March 5: Reichstag elections. Nazis and their nationalist allies win a slim majority.

March 24: Reichstag passes the Enabling Law, giving Hitler dictatorial powers.

December 1: Nazi party is made the only lawful party in Germany.

1934—**June 30:** The "Night of Long Knives" begins. Ernst Röhm and others are executed.

August 2: Death of President Hindenburg. Hitler declares himself the absolute ruler of the German nation.

1935—Germany begins drafting men into military service.

1936—German troops enter the Rhineland in violation of the Treaty of Versailles.

1938—**March 13:** Anschluss. Germany annexes Austria.

September 29: Munich Agreement surrenders the Sudentenland to Germany.

1939—**March 19:** Germany takes control of the rest of Czechoslovakia.

August 23: Germany signs a nonaggression pact with the Soviet Union.

September 1: Germany invades Poland. World War II begins.

1945—**January 27:** Soviet troops liberate the Auschwitz concentration camp.

April 30: Adolf Hitler commits suicide in an underground bunker in Berlin.

May 8: Victory in Europe Day; fighting in Europe ends.

August 15: Japan surrenders to Allies.

September 2: Armistice officially ends World War II.

1951—Israel creates Holocaust Memorial Day.

2015—Auschwitz survivors mark the seventieth anniversary of liberation.

CHAPTER NOTES

CHAPTER 1. Germany and the First War

1. "Comments of the German Delegation to the Paris Peace Conference on the Conditions of Peace, Oct., 1919," International Conciliation, October 1919, http://www.bibliobase.com/history/research_companion/primary_sources/world/generic/chapters/chapter7.xml (accessed July 10, 2015).
2. Adolf Hitler, *Mein Kampf*, trans. Ralph Manheim (Boston: Houghton Mifflin, 1971), 19–20.
3. August Kubizek, *The Young Hitler I Knew: The Memoirs of Hitler's Childhood Friend*, trans. Geoffrey Brooks (New York: Arcade, 2011), Kindle ed., loc. 2593, 2627.
4. Hitler, 123.
5. Ibid., 223.
6. Jan Fleischhauer, "New German Biography: Hitler's Underestimated Charisma," *Spiegel Online International*, October 11, 2013, http://www.spiegel.de/international/germany/historian-interview-new-book-explores-personal-charm-of-hitler-a-927155.html.

CHAPTER 2. The Party That Hitler Built

1. "Program of the German Workers' Party (1920)," *German History in Documents and Images*, vol. 6, Weimar Germany, 1918/19–1933, http://germanhistorydocs.ghi-dc.org/sub_document.cfm?document_id=3910.
2. Peter Neville, *Mussolini*, 2nd ed. (London: Routledge, 2014) 49.
3. Richard Koenigsberg, "Ideologies of War: Nationalism, Nazism, Genocide," Library of Social Science, November 2013, http://blog.libraryofsocialscience.com.
4. "Social Democratic Platform," *Facing History and Ourselves*, https://www.facinghistory.org/weimar-republic-fragility-democracy/politics/social-democratic-party-platform-politics-political-party (accessed June 26, 2015).
5. Nazi Germany Quotations, *Alpha History*, 2014, http://alphahistory.com/nazigermany/nazi-germany-quotations/.
6. Heinrich Himmler, *Jewish Virtual Library*, https://www.jewishvirtuallibrary.org/jsource/Holocaust/himmler.html (accessed June 6, 2015).

7. Adolf Hitler, *Mein Kampf*, trans. Ralph Manheim (Boston: Houghton Mifflin, 1971), 134.

CHAPTER 3. Hitler's Revolt

1. Harold J. Gordon, *Hitler and the Beer Hall Putsch* (Princeton, NJ: Princeton University Press, 2015), 288.
2. "Adolf Hitler Attempts a Coup, 1923," *EyeWitness to History*, 2005, http://www.eyewitnesstohistory.com/putsch.htm.
3. C.N. Trueman, "The Beer Hall Putsch of 1923," *HistoryLearningSite*, May 22, 2015, http://www.historylearningsite.co.uk/?s=beer+hall+putsch.
4. "Hitler's Speech at the Putsch Trial (February 1924)," *German History in Documents and Images*, http://germanhistorydocs.ghi-dc.org/sub_document.cfm?document_id=3913 (accessed June 27, 2015).
5. "A Letter to Adolf Hitler, Oct. 7, 1923," *World Future Fund*, http://www.worldfuturefund.org (accessed June 27, 2015).

CHAPTER 4. Politics and Power

1. "Rohm, Ernst," Yad Vashem, Shoah Resource Center, The International School for Holocaust Studies, http://www.yadvashem.org/odot_pdf/Microsoft%20Word%20-%205832.pdf (accessed June 6, 2015).
2. C.N. Trueman, "Paul von Hindenburg," *HistoryLearningSite*, May 22, 2015, http://www.historylearningsite.co.uk/?s=paul+von+hindenburg.
3. "Nazi Conspiracy and Aggression: Individual Responsibility of Defendants: Franz Von Papen," *The Nizkor Project*, 1991-2012, http://www.nizkor.org/hweb/imt/nca/nca-02/nca-02-16-responsibility-18-02-04.html.
4. "Hitler Forms His First Government," *Manchester Guardian*, January 31, 1933, http://www.theguardian.com/theguardian/2011/jan/31/archive-hitler-forms-first-government.
5. Lily Rothman, "Who Started the Reichstag Fire?" *Time*, February 27, 2015, time.com/3717003/reichstag-fire-1933/.
6. "Minutes of the Conference of Ministers on March 7, 1933," *German History in Documents and Images*, http://germanhistorydocs.ghi-dc.org/pdf/eng/English4_new.pdf (accessed June 28, 2015).

7. William L. Shirer, *The Rise and Fall of the Third Reich* (New York: Fawcett Publications, 1962), 308.

CHAPTER 5. The Führer's War

1. "Adolf Hitler—Speech at Hindenburg's Funeral in Tannenberg Monument," *World Future Fund*, http://der-fuehrer.org/reden/english/34-08-07.htm (accessed June 29, 2015).
2. C.N. Trueman, "The Fuehrer Principle," *HistoryLearningSite*, March 9, 2015, http://www.historylearningsite.co.uk/?s=fuhrer+principle.
3. Sebastian Haffner, *Defying Hitler: A Memoir*, trans. Oliver Pretzl (Plunkett Lake Press, 2014), Kindle ed., loc. 356.
4. C.N. Trueman, "Germany and Rearmament," *HistoryLearningSite*, April 28, 2015, http://www.historylearningsite.co.uk/?s=germany+and+rearmament.
5. Jim Lindsay, "The Munich Agreement," History Lesson, Video, September 16, 2012, https://www.youtube.com/watch?v=wKA-lhWFbsE.
6. "1939: Germany Invades Poland," *BBC News*, September 1, 1939, http://news.bbc.co.uk/onthisday/hi/dates/stories/september/1/newsid_3506000/3506335.stm (accessed June 30, 2015).
7. "Ohrdruf," *Holocaust Encyclopedia*, United States Holocaust Memorial Museum, 2014, http://www.ushmm.org/wlc/en/article.php?ModuleId=10006131#seealso.
8. Camilla Turner, "Holocaust Memorial Day: Survivors Return to Auschwitz," *The Telegraph*, June 27, 2015, http://www.telegraph.co.uk/history/world-war-two/11370854/Holocaust-Memorial-Day-survivors-return-to-Auschwitz.html.
9. "Auschwitz 70th Anniversary: Survivors Warn of New Crimes," *BBC News*, January 27, 2015, http://www.bbc.com/news/world-europe-30996555.

GLOSSARY

Allies—During World War II, the group of nations headed by Great Britain and later joined by the United States and the Soviet Union.

anti-Semitism—Hatred of, or discrimination against, Jews as a group.

appeasement—The act of giving something to an aggressive power to keep the peace.

Aryan—Nazi term for Nordic, or Northern European, peoples.

Axis—During World War II, the group of nations headed by Germany and opposing the Allies.

chancellor—Head of State in a parliamentary government.

Communism—A form of government in which property is communally owned.

decree—A formal and authoritative order.

fascism—A one-party system of government in which society is controlled by military force, secret police, and censorship.

genetics—The science dealing with inherited characteristics of life forms.

genocide—The systematic extermination, or attempted extermination, of an entire racial, ethnic, political, or religious group.

German Workers' Party—The political party that became the foundation of the Nazi party.

Gestapo *(Geheime-Staats-Polizei)*—A secret state police agency in Nazi Germany.

Holocaust—Originally, an all-consuming fire. Used to describe the extermination of more than eleven million people, including six million Jews.

lebensraum ("living space")—Nazi term for expansion of German territory.

master race—Nazi term for Germanic peoples who were regarded as superior to all other races.

Nazi party—National Socialist German Workers' Party. The party of Adolf Hitler.

platform—In politics, a statement of basic principles.

police state—A government in which the will of a dictatorial regime is enforced by police agencies possessing broad powers.

propaganda—A presentation of ideas slanted to shape and control public opinion.

putsch—An uprising or rebellion from within.

rabble-rouser—A person with the ability to sway masses of people in a particular direction.

racial hygiene—The idea of protecting the genetic health of a people through selective breeding and other measures.

racism—An irrational belief in the superiority of a given group, based upon inborn racial traits.

Reichstag—The German parliament, or legislative body.

reparations—Money that a country or group that loses a war pays because of the damage, injury, deaths, etc., it has caused.

SA *(Sturmabteilung)*—("Stormtroopers") In the early days of the Nazi party, a private army used to intimidate and control enemies. Often called "Brownshirts" after the color of their uniforms.

SS *(Shutzstaffel)*—("Protection squad") The elite guard of the Nazi state. It administered the Final Solution and insured obedience to the dictates of the Führer.

sterilize—To deprive of the ability to produce offspring.

swastika—The hooked cross symbol of the Nazi party.

Thousand-Year Reich—Hitler's name for the empire that he vowed would last a thousand years.

Treaty of Versailles—The formal agreement that ended World War I.

Valhalla—Norse mythology: The great hall of dead heroes.

warrant—A legal order permitting arrest, search, or seizure of property.

Wehrmacht—The armed services of Germany.

FURTHER READING

Books

Giblin, James Cross. *The Life and Death of Adolf Hitler.* New York: HMH Books for Young Readers, 2015.

Hoose, Phillip. *The Boys Who Challenged Hitler: Knud Pedersen and the Churchill Club.* New York: Farrar, Strauss and Giroux (BYR), 2015.

Rausch, Georg. *Unlikely Warrior: A Jewish Soldier in Hitler's Army.* New York: Farrar, Strauss and Giroux (BYR), 2015.

Skog, Jason. *The Legacy of the Holocaust.* Mankato, MN: Compass Point Books. 2011.

Warren, Andreas. *Surviving Hitler: A Boy in the Nazi Death Camps.* New York: HarperCollins, 2013.

Websites

BBC Bitesize (Hitler and the Nazis)

www.bbc.co.uk/search?filter=bitesize&q=Hitler%20and%20Nazis

Includes detailed information for students about the rise of Hitler and the Nazis.

Yad Vashem Video Toolbox

www.yadvashem.org/yv/en/education/video/index.asp

Provides videos of analysis and testimonies about the Holocaust.

United States Holocaust Memorial Museum

www.ushmm.org

Includes background information, personal histories, photographs, artifacts, and film footage from the Holocaust.

INDEX

Index